Downshifting Made Easy

How to plan for your planet-friendly future

Downshifting
Made Easy

How to plan for
your planet-friendly future

Marian Van Eyk McCain

BOOKS

Winchester, UK
Washington, USA

First published by O-Books, 2011
O Books is an imprint of John Hunt Publishing Ltd., The Bothy, Deershot Lodge, Park Lane, Ropley,
Hants, SO24 0BE, UK
office1@o-books.net
www.o-books.com

For distributor details and how to order please visit the 'Ordering' section on our website.

Text copyright: Marian Van Eyk McCain 2010

ISBN: 978 1 84694 541 0

A CIP catalogue record for this book is available from the British Library.

Design: Lee Nash

Printed in the UK by CPI Antony Rowe
Printed in the USA by Offset Paperback Mfrs, Inc

We operate a distinctive and ethical publishing philosophy in all
areas of our business, from our global network of authors to
production and worldwide distribution.

CONTENTS

Chapter 6. The 'who?' questions

Chapter 7. All the nitty-gritty bits

For Gaia

"An inspiring and readable book that not only offers a practical framework but also gives valuable insights into the process step by step. Marian speaks from experience, but adds the warm dimension of the heart, making downshifting not only desirable but more easily achievable."

Maddy Harland, Editor of 'Permaculture Magazine: inspiration for sustainable living' - www.permaculture.co.uk

"Marian's new book 'Downshifting Made Easy' is a great addition to the simplicity field. Based on an approach that includes grounding yourself and your life in a deep connection with Nature — including the systems that sustain all life, and the true nature of your own being — Marian's book provides you with a set of core principles and penetrating questions that will help you create real and lasting satisfaction. Her writing style mirrors her approach, it is simple, humorous in many places and grounded in the important ecological issues of our time. I highly recommend it."

Bruce Elkin, Life Coach. Author of 'Simplicity and Success' - www.BruceElkin.com

"Marian does a wonderful job of combining the practical with the philosophical, inspiring us to experience life to the fullest. She reminds us of the importance of making conscious decisions that free us from the manipulation of the consumer society: the importance of remembering that all of life is connected: and the significance of the fact that we're building a way of life that is more delightful and satisfying than life in the cutthroat consumer society. She reminds us to ask: 'What is your life consecrated to?' The answer will determine your happiness and wellbeing."

Cecile Andrews, Author of 'Circle of Simplicity', 'Slow is Beautiful', and 'Less is More' - www.cecileandrews.com

Introduction

I keep six honest serving-men
(They taught me all I knew);
Their names are What and Why and When
And How and Where and Who.
Rudyard Kipling (from *Just So Stories*, 1902)

More and more people are doing it these days. It's a trend. And if you picked up this book, then you are either doing it too or at the very least thinking about doing it. In which case, you are the very person for whom I wrote this book.

The book is all about downshifting—what it is, who does it, how to prepare for it, when and where and how to do it and why it is so important in the greater scheme of things.

Simply put, 'downshifting' means moving to a simpler, less stressful lifestyle, becoming less dependent on the consumer culture and—hopefully—setting up, for oneself and one's family, some protection against the very real possibility of future economic problems, shortages of resources and probably some social chaos. (We shall be looking at this definition again in Chapter 1.)

It also, for most of the people who do it, involves becoming happier, more relaxed, more healthy and more deeply satisfied with life. Furthermore, of you are a downshifter—or a potential downshifter—you are part of what is arguably the most important evolutionary process that we human beings have taken part in since we stopped being hunter-gatherers and started building settlements.

Some of us downshift because we want to, for a variety of reasons, either personal, like wanting more time for family, or ethical, like deciding to reduce our 'eco-footprint'. Others downshift because they are forced to, also for a number of different reasons, often unhappy ones like the loss of a loved one or being laid off from a well-paying job.

Whilst our starting point in each of these cases is different, the tasks we face are usually quite similar. The first task is *thinking about the process*: its pros and cons, its implications—not only practical but psychological, emotional and social also—and all its whys and wherefores. In other words, the what, why, when, how, where and who of it.

Furthermore, each of those 'honest serving-men' can be examined at one or more levels, such as:

the outer level (practicalities)
the inner level (feeling)
the deeper level (how each question relates to what is going on in the wider world and to philosophy of life and belief systems)

Unlike many other books on the subject, this one focuses on all three of these levels, and particularly on the second and third, for reasons that will become increasingly evident as you read on.

If you are a potential downshifter, my hope is that by the time you have finished reading you will have not only a framework for better understanding the 'big picture issues' involved here but also a guiding set of principles to apply in your own situation and a clear idea of what to do next.

Above all, I hope you will find it useful to take this time out for pondering on the topic and that by doing so you will find inspiration, motivation and a keenness to take the next step in your journey.

I am going to use some rather weird shorthand in this book. Words like 'sustainable' and 'unsustainable' take longer to type and make me sound like one of those boring leaflets put out by environmental organizations with too much grant money to spend. So instead of 'sustainable' I'll be using the word 'green'.

'Unsustainable' will be replaced by 'gray': gray, like dusk, when the sun has set, night is approaching and everything is beginning to fade towards black. Because if the carbon in the atmosphere rises to 400 parts per million and beyond and the oil and water run out, our lovely, green and blue and gold planet *will* be fading towards black.

You'd think every one of us would have turned at least light green by now, wouldn't you? Why haven't we? We'll look at that question in more depth in later chapters and I'll try to supply some useful answers.

It would be surprising if there really was anybody left in total ignorance of the environmental crisis we are facing, since the media are full of stories about it these days. But your average daily newspaper is quite likely to run a story about global warming, another about some species of furry creature that has just joined the endangered species list and a third about how disappointed the retailers are because the Christmas sales figures were down a notch. And not a word about the deep connection between these three stories. No joining of the dots. Example: a neighbor sitting near me on the bus one day was loudly lamenting the closure of yet another little local food store that we had just passed. And even as she did so, she was clutching on her lap a plastic bag full of stuff from the super-market whose entrance into the area had been one of the primary reasons that many small stores, unable to compete, had gone out of business. She is a highly intelligent woman, but obviously not good at joining dots. I think this is why there are so many people who have not yet turned green. It is not that they don't know about the problems our species is facing. It is not that they are in denial. It is not that they know but don't care. It is that they haven't really joined all the dots together yet. They haven't really got it that it is we ordinary folk who hold in our hands the power to change things, to live differently, to turn green and to create a new, satisfying way of life for everyone on the planet before it is too late. So I am going to talk more about dot-joining in Chapter 4. Dot-joining is the key to the 'how' section. And if this book is to be of practical use it needs to give its readers a handle on that 'how' question.

Human beings are complex creatures. We don't just eat and sleep and procreate. We don't just deal with the practical aspects of our lives. There are many layers to our beingness. We conceptualize, visualize, analyze, strategize and plan. As well as ideas and concepts, we have feelings, hang-ups and deep-seated beliefs. Some of us meditate. Some of us pray. Some of us worship. Some of us are in service to ideals and entities that we experience as greater and more important than our personal selves.

When we are contemplating lifestyle changes, we must take these other aspects of ourselves into consideration as well as the practical ones. For it is the emotional layers of our lives that give us feedback about whether or not we are moving in the right direction. And it is the spiritual levels of ourselves that invest our lives with meaning. Without meaning, we are mere robots.

So each of the questions we need to consider about downshifting—the what, why, when, how, where and who questions—needs be looked at through the lens of practicality, of our feelings and emotions, and of our spirituality.

I hope that as you make your way from the hands of one 'honest serving-man' to the next you will glean some helpful insights, not only into the nature of downshifting but into your own motivation, your beliefs and maybe even your fears and doubts. You will also, I hope, pick up some practical hints on how to achieve your goal of living more greenly and lightly on the Earth. And at the end, you will find suggestions for other books and resources that I think may be helpful.

Finally, I shall leave you with a set of core principles which you can use as a guide.

My greatest hope is that by the time you have finished reading the book you will feel inspired, reassured and confident that you are on the right path. And the very fact that you are reading it means you have taken a step on that path already.

Chapter 1

The 'what?' questions

What do we mean by 'downshifting'?

We need to begin with a look at what downshifting *isn't*. Let's get that out of the way first.

For one thing, it does *not* mean you have to move from the city to the country, buy green rubber boots and slosh around in the mud chasing chickens. (Though if that is what you have always yearned to do, then by all means go for it.)

In fact it doesn't mean you have to move anywhere. Unless the bailiffs are right now knocking on your door, you can start the downshifting process exactly where you are and stay there.

It doesn't necessarily mean that you have to manage on a lower income, though for the majority of downshifters that is part of it, at least at first. And for the *in*voluntary downshifters, it is usually a given.

It probably won't mean that you are less busy. Of course if you have become one of those 80-hours a week corporate types who is a slave to your company, your boss and your BlackBerry, it may well result in less busyness. But for many people, downshifting simply means that you exchange one kind of busyness—the kind that leaves you stressed, tired and anxious—for the kind that sees you falling happily into bed each night with the satisfying feeling of a day's work well done.

Most people, if you ask them what downshifting is, will tell you that is it about giving up things, earning less, dropping to a lower standard of living, getting rid of clutter and going without some of the things that have made your life comfortable in the past.

That is not an accurate description. Sure, the process of

downshifting may well involve getting rid of clutter. But apart from the most dedicated packrats among us, most of us don't really *like* clutter anyway. And we enjoy the freedom that decluttering brings.[1] It is just that we usually don't get around to doing it. So once we decide to downshift, then clearing out our drawers and closets, the attic, the basement, the garage etc can be a good place to begin. The benefit is as much psychological as anything else. It makes us feel good. It underlines our determination to make a 'new start' and by lightening our load of 'stuff' we are making a symbolic statement about the overall need to lighten our load and lighten our impact on the planet that is our home. Decluttering doesn't, in itself, make much difference to the world around us, except inasmuch as it provides new resources for other people in the form of inexpensive, second-hand goods. And that is an important contribution. But the value of decluttering as a starting-place and as a symbolic statement of our intention is huge. And the surprisingly good feeling that comes after a good decluttering session acts like a sort of yeast in the dough of our lives. By making us realize that possessions weigh us down and how little 'stuff' we actually *need* to live a full and contented and productive life, it starts the slow, subtle process of attitude change that is the key to successful downshifting.

As for the other things—the giving-up, the lowering of standards, loss of income and going without—those are *not* what downshifting is really all about.

OK, so what is it, then?

Downshifting means shifting down into a closer, more satisfying, more meaningful relationship with the Earth, with the ground beneath your feet, and with Nature, which also includes your own biology and your own true nature. Downshifting means moving into a closer relationship with the really important and meaningful things in life—things that give you true and permanent satisfaction instead of temporary and illusory satisfaction.

It means becoming more aware of your surroundings, more aware of the weather, the movements of sun and moon and stars, the cycle of the seasons and the basic needs of your life: clean air, pure water, food and what is needed for cooking and eating it, shelter, clothes, energy for cooking and heating, and transport from place to place.

It also means learning as much as you can about your own impact on the Earth and whether you are taking more than your share of what the Earth provides. That's because the central point of downshifting is to balance your own needs (and unless you're single, your family's needs) with the needs of other life forms and the needs of the planet as a whole and to make sure that the balance is a fair one all around.

I find it useful to think of it in terms of the gears in a car. When you are driving a car, you shift down to a lower gear in order to get more power and more traction. One result is that you go more slowly. Which in many cases is necessary, for example when going round corners or going downhill. And in some cases is inevitable, like for instance when you are climbing *uphill*.

Downshifting your lifestyle is remarkably similar. Right now, there is a lot of power in the hands of 'gray' people and organizations. But as things change—and they are already starting to change, as we can see from the way the weather is becoming more turbulent and unpredictable and from the fact that more and more types of animals and plants are joining the endangered species list—the power those people have, a lot of which is based on ample supplies of oil, is going to wane. And the people who are downshifting to green will find their power steadily rising. For when you have the power to feed and clothe yourself and your local shops and farms and artisans are thriving so well that you can obtain whatever you need locally, you have an enormous amount of power.

And think about traction. Traction means gripping the ground: holding on to the earth. Holding on to our precious

Planet Earth. Living *within* Nature and in harmony with its laws rather than kidding ourselves we can be independent from it.

Going green means living more slowly. Which means enjoying your life more: sipping it and savoring it instead of gulping each moment so fast that you don't really taste it.

And we *are* going round a corner. You can't see round corners and nobody knows for sure, yet, how the climate change thing is going to pan out. It may get so warm in England that we'll find oranges and lemons growing in Sussex and hoopoes coming to the garden feeders in Liverpool. Or the Gulf Stream might be forced to stop flowing, the British Isles will get much colder and the British will get so good at ice hockey that they end up beating the Canadians.

When you are going downhill too fast, which we are in so many ways, with the polar ice caps melting, fish stocks dwindling, coral reefs dying and all kinds of other scary changes happening, downshifting gears is a must. By the same token, there is a huge amount that needs to change and making all those necessary changes feels like starting on a very uphill climb. But we can do it. You can do it. I hope this book will encourage, inspire and empower you so that you can truly feel that even though our planet has a problem, you are now becoming part of the solution.

What are your feelings about downshifting?

What sort of feelings, ideas, thoughts etc arise in you as you read these first pages? Sit quietly, close your eyes for a moment and check in with your body. Let it tell you what emotions are aroused when you think about downshifting.

What do you feel? Is it excitement? (*Wow, this is going to be good, I'm on my way at last!*) Dread? (*Oh no, do I really have to do this? It's going to be awful.*) Distaste? (*Yuk, this probably means I'm supposed to give away all my possessions and live on potato peelings or something.*) Resentment? (*It's not fair! Why me?*) Fear? (*What if I can't do it? Would that make me a bad person?*) Curiosity? (*Where's she going with all this feely stuff?*) Fascination? (*Hey, this might be an interesting experiment to try.*) Cynicism? (*Oh yeah, the same old crap I suppose.*) Eagerness? (*I'll start clearing out the garage right after lunch!*)

We are not like machines. We are living, breathing, feeling creatures. So everything in our lives has a feeling component as well as a practical one. Therefore, it is important always to pay attention to what is going on inside you as well as what is going on outside. Let's start by looking at what sorts of feelings you can be likely to expect when you actually embark on a downshift.

Everyone who decides to downshift does so for a reason. And the reason has to be an important one for the person who's making it because changing one's life around isn't always easy. We'll be looking at some of the reasons—the 'why' of downshifting—in the next chapter. All I want to say now about the 'why' is that there are as many different reasons for making the decision to downshift as there are people making it. However, there is always a feeling of some sort behind it. And many of these feelings are similar, regardless of the actual reason. Whether you decide to change your lifestyle because you are sick of being part of the corporate rat-race and you want to step down into a saner, more peaceful and relaxed way of living, or whether it is because you want a healthier life for your family, a smaller mortgage to support, or a smaller eco-footprint, no matter what it is there will probably be a feeling of some kind of leaning or straining forward into the future. It is a feeling that may be as mild as anticipation or as strong as longing, or even as severe as desperation.

If you find yourself forced into downshifting there will be a whole bunch of feelings to get through even before you start to plan the future—grief, anger, resentment, guilt, the feelings that always come, in some measure, with any kind of loss. It may be necessary to do some short-term decision-making during this adjustment period, but crisis changes us, sometimes in unexpected ways. So if possible, don't make any long-term plans while you are still dealing with any of those kinds of emotions.

Once the decision has been made and announced, there is often a swelling of joy—even euphoria. Most of us dislike indecision. We feel relief when the decision is made and a there is a sense of forward movement. Even if you are doing it from necessity, once you have moved out of crisis mode and started to plan your future, the same thing can happen. There's a feeling of setting sail, of catching a breeze, and the adventurer in us relishes that feeling.

But there's a slight danger here. When we have been looking at a problem for a while and have finally decided that the solution demands some decisive—even drastic—action, most of us tend to start believing that the action, whatever it is, will be the solution to *all* our problems. We run the risk of piling all our emotional eggs into that one basket. I am talking rose-colored glasses here. Because no matter what sort of lifestyle we have chosen, whether high-tech or low-tech, urban or rural, solitary or communal, high maintenance or low maintenance, there will probably be issues of one kind or another. (Unless of course we have been meditating so long that we've become fully enlightened and nothing ever bothers us any more.) For most ordinary mortals, life throws up issues on a regular basis. It's just that different lifestyles involve different issues. But when there's a big change ahead, for a while we can kid ourselves that once the change is made it will be Shangri-La. Wrong! However, that's OK, because we need the motivation. We need to believe that the change will solve all our problems. That helps us to jump the hurdles involved in actually *making* the change. So it is alright to feel the longing, because it helps to push us into the change. It is alright to feel the pleasure and anticipation and to wear the rose-colored glasses for a while because that helps to carry us through the change.

Big changes also, for most of us, bring with them a certain amount of anticipatory fear. And that's alright too. Just think of it as stage fright. Most people get that. Just breathe through it.

In any case, the way to deal with *any* feeling is not to try and deny it or to push it away, even if you don't like it, but to acknowledge it—at least to oneself—and accept it as part and parcel of the process. It is important to say 'yes' to it. Say to yourself, "*Here am I, yearning/feeling excited/feeling fearful…this is the truth of this here, now moment.*" Develop what spiritual teachers have called The Observing Self—a part of you that sits on your own shoulder, watching but not interfering. Just saying "*Hmmm…that's interesting…*"

One of the trickier feelings to deal with—and one that often pops up in the context of downshifting—is doubt. Sudden setbacks, things not working out exactly as you anticipated or hoped or wanted, the reality kicking in once bridges are burned… many things can bring on the doubts. "*Oh why did we ever decide to do this…?*" Moving to a smaller house and discovering that Grandma's sideboard won't even fit through the front door ("*I thought you measured it*"/ "*You said YOU would measure it!*"), the children hating the new school, termites in the wall, the clayey soil that's so different from the loam in your old garden, unexpected dental problems and no decent dentist for miles around…the list of potential setbacks is endless. Every personal account I have ever read of downshifting people or families involves stories of these initial difficulties and the doubt, regret, even terror that they caused. And this phase can last quite a while. But not forever.

Homesickness may be part of the package too, especially in the initial stages, and even people whose downshifting doesn't involve physically moving house can feel it just as strongly. For example, those who make a vow not to buy anything except actual essentials—like food—for a whole year often find themselves looking back wistfully, at first, to the days when they used to buy anything that took their fancy. Loss of any kind causes a measure of grief. I remember when I gave up smoking at the age of 26 how I mourned for many weeks the disappearance of that pleasurable 'hit' from a freshly-lit cigarette. For a little while, all the fun seemed to go out of my life. After many smoke-free decades, that seems utterly crazy to me now. But it felt very real at the time.

Once again, the trick is not to try and stave off those feelings, or to try and rationalize yourself out of them. And certainly don't beat up on yourself for having them. Just say 'yes' to them. Breathe through them. Say "*Here am I, feeling nostalgic for what used to be.*" And that's alright. Remember the famous inscription inside King Solomon's ring? "This, too, shall pass." It does. Humans have this innate ability to adjust, physically and emotionally. Your new, downshifted life, strange at first and redolent with all kinds of new feelings, will sooner or later become the new normal. And only when it has will you find yourself one day realizing, as so many thousands of people before you have realized, that you are actually a lot happier now than you were in your old life. Because you see, the process is not only a practical one and an emotional one. It is also a spiritual one.

What are the 'deeper' aspects of downshifting?

In other words, what does it have to do with philosophies and belief systems?

Theologian Thomas Berry, who died in 2009, used to say, "The Universe is a communion of subjects, not a collection of objects." In other words, we are not really separate from each other, even though we might sometimes feel as though we are. Even though we, unlike trees, are free to move around on the surface of the Earth, which inevitably gives us a feeling of separateness, it is just an illusion. We are as much a part of the Earth as fish are a part of the ocean. In ways that seem mysterious to us because our sense organs cannot detect them, everything that exists is intimately connected.

Scientist Alain Aspect and his colleagues conducted a famous experiment in Paris in 1982, which has been repeated many times since. In this experiment, two particles were fired from the same place in two different directions, both spinning, and when the direction of spin on one particle was changed, the other, though not connected in any known way, changed its spin to match, faster than the speed of light. These experiments and many other experiments and discoveries in quantum physics have completely revolutionized our understanding of what the Universe is like and what it is made of. Unfortunately, the science is way ahead of our cultural habits and we continue to behave in many ways as though the Earth were flat and did not really go around the sun. (And as though the Earth were nothing but a big cookie jar specially put there to satisfy human desires. But let's not get into that right now...)

Most of all, what quantum physics has taught us is that, contrary to the so-called 'certainties' of the old scientists like Newton and Descartes, the more we find out about the Universe the less we really know. It seems that much of it is so mysterious and unknowable that it is doubtful we shall ever really understand it.

So instead of being puffed up with that old, 'know-it-all' sense of self-importance that humanity has had in the past, it is time for humility. And for reverence towards those great mysteries that are so much bigger and vaster than our puny, finite, human minds can comprehend.

Humility and acceptance go together. And these are key, spiritual values. Many great spiritual traditions—Christianity, Islam, Judaism, Hinduism, Buddhism, and most of the traditions of indigenous cultures, such as the Native Americans—have humility and acceptance as part of their belief structure. In religion, the whole notion of worship, whether it be the worship of a God, a Goddess, the sun, a mountain, a Nature spirit or whatever, is about bowing our heads in front of something greater and more mysterious than ourselves and yet something with which we are intimately connected and by which we are embraced.

So-called 'worship' can often be a hollow ritual. But if we are lucky, there are special moments in all our lives when a feeling of reverence and awe and a sense of profound connectedness with all-that-is breaks through into our ordinary consciousness in a sudden and unexpected way. This may happen at fairly predictable times, such as when we are listening to beautiful music, watching a sunset, or being present at the birth of a child. But it can also happen at what seem like random times. Although frequently there is some association with the outdoors. For the Japanese farmer Masanobu Fukuoka, it happened while he was watching a skein of geese honking their way across the sky. For a friend of mine, it happened while he was lying on his back in long grass, watching the grass stems moving in the breeze. It happened to me the first time, when I was a young teenager, standing under a blossoming cherry tree. Psychologist Abraham Maslow called these 'peak experiences'.[2] And when they start to happen more frequently, it is a sign that we are moving into the phase of our development that he called 'self-actualization'. (I shall be saying a little more about Maslow and his ideas in the next section.)

The reason I am talking about this here is that people who downshift to simpler lifestyles usually find themselves living closer to the Earth in some way, closer to their true, biological needs and natures rather than to the artificial structures of the culture. And it seems that the more we do that, the more likely we are to have these peak experiences.

Downshifting, you see, leads to spiritual growth. And once you are on the path of spiritual growth you are unlikely ever to get off it again. You won't want to.

Chapter 2

The 'why?' questions

Why does anyone need to downshift?

I have already mentioned some of the reasons why humanity, as a whole, needs to start living within its means. I know these are painful things to think about. And it also gets tedious to have to hear about them again if you are already aware of the facts. But just for readers who may not be up to speed with all this, I will briefly go through them here. If you are already very well-versed in all this, just bear with me. It won't take long.

We all know what happens if you consistently spend more than you earn. The utility companies cut off your electricity and your telephone, your car gets repossessed, the bank forecloses on your mortgage, or if you are renting, your landlord throws you out. Eventually you get so deeply into debt that there is no alternative but to declare bankruptcy. Well, for quite a while now, we humans have been spending the Earth's resources at a faster rate than the Earth can produce them. Things like oil, coal, peat, gas etc which we get out of the ground took millions of years to accumulate and we have already used so much of all of these that it will not be long before they run out. We have taken fish from the sea faster than fish can breed, so soon there will be none left at all. And in trying to feed so many people, food producers have gotten into the habit of using the sort of methods that maximize their yields but also impoverish the soil so that the foods many people eat today, even the fruit and vegetables, have less nutritional value than the same foods had in our grandparents' day. That food is also—unless it is organically grown—likely to contain traces of pesticides and herbicides and other chemicals potentially damaging to our health.

There is no way we can replace the oil and coal and gas etc. Once they are gone, they are gone. However, the services they have rendered to us—such as getting us from place to place, keeping us warm and lighting our houses—can equally well be provided by things that *don't* run out, such as the wind and the tides and the sunshine.

So there are three separate issues here. One is the depletion of natural, non-renewable resources, and another is the mess we have made while using them (not only a physical mess in terms of pollution but also a sociological mess in terms of all the inequalities and injustices our global systems have created). The third is the fact that our numbers are growing very fast. Which means there is less and less to go round and also that we are taking up the space—and the food—that rightfully belongs to all the other creatures with whom we are supposed to be sharing this planet.

Fair Shares

Environmental scientists have worked out a certain figure that you get by dividing up all the land in the world that is capable of producing food and sharing it out equally amongst all the human beings in the world. They have also calculated how many parts per million of carbon the air can hold and still be healthy to breathe and what is the amount of productive land and sea area required to sequester carbon dioxide emissions and absorb other waste products harmlessly. After some careful, mathematical calculation, they have come up with a figure which stands for the optimum size of an 'ecological footprint'.[3] It comes out at somewhere around 2.1gha (which stands for 'global hectares'). In other words, if everybody in the world had an ecological footprint of 2.1gha (or ideally, a little bit less, to allow for the fact that world population is still increasing), there would be enough for everyone, life would chug along really nicely and the whole world would be green instead of gray. We would be out of debt.

At the moment, the average ecological footprint of human beings the world over is more than 2.7. I say 'more than' because it takes a couple of years for the figures to be recalculated, the last report was in 2008 and the figure has been rising slightly each year.

You might think that being 0.6 over the target is not too bad. But what we must remember is that we are talking about the whole world here. So every year, by September, we have already overshot the carrying capacity of our planet for that calendar year. And every year, what they call 'world overshoot day' happens earlier and earlier. Even more importantly, we need to remember that the 2.7 average reported in 2008 included Sierra Leone and other African countries *where thousands starve to death*.

There are a few places, such as Bolivia and Albania, where the average eco-footprint is spot on, at 2.1. However, in the UK, the average is 5.3gha. And in the USA it is a whopping 9.4, the highest in the world except for the United Arab Emirates (9.5). Australia comes in at 7.8, New Zealand at 7.7 and Canada at 7.1. The Western European countries range from 4.1 in Germany, to 8 in Denmark.

So it is in all these 'well off' countries that changes need to happen and people need to downshift, as a matter of urgency, if our planet is to remain habitable for our children and grand-children and the generations to come.

But please don't panic. You must not imagine for one moment that for us all to have the 'right' sort of footprint we would all have to live in the edge of starvation. Because that's absolutely not true. You see, the real culprit is inequality.

Inequality
Believe it or not, the richest tenth of the world's population have a greater negative environmental impact than *all the rest put together*.

Cuba, which is one of the most highly egalitarian countries in the world, has a footprint of only 1.8 gha and yet, according the UN's Human Development Index, in 2006 it was the only country to achieve both sustainability and good quality lives for *all* its people.[4]

The biggest problem with inequality is not just that the super-rich are gobbling up far more than their fair share. It is that by living lives of 'conspicuous consumption' they set an example that everyone else wants to emulate. Thus gradually, over the years, the bar gets steadily raised so that yesterday's luxuries become today's 'necessities'. So the problem is not so much with the mansions of the super-rich but with the millions of 'McMansions' built in an attempt to emulate them. Thorstein Veblen, way back in 1899, called this process 'emulative consumption' and it is largely that which has driven those footprint averages up so high in Western countries.[5]

That is the first answer to the 'why' question. But there are two more answers, which we shall turn to now.

Why downshifting will probably make you happier.
We have looked at what I call the 'big picture' (sociological) reasons. But when people ask me, "Why do I need to downshift?" there is another set of reasons I give them too—the emotional ones. That's because everybody I know who really has downshifted to a simpler way of life and has stuck with it has become happier than they were before—*everyone*! And that is most certainly true of me as well.

In my book *The Lilypad List: 7 steps to the simple life*,[6] I told many stories about my own adventures in simple living and the various forms it has taken in my lifetime, from homesteading in the Australian bush to living in an inner-city apartment in San Francisco to the ancient cob cottage in rural England that I live in now. By describing my own adventures and discoveries, I hoped to show that there are many ways to live 'the good life' in a simple way and that the important thing is to work out the one

best suited to you, as an individual and—if you have a family—
to the family as a whole. I want to stress that here also.
Downshifting is a process that is infinitely adaptable, so your
starting point is not about saving money, managing on less,
doing without or any of those rather unpleasant-sounding
things. It is not about taking nasty medicine. It is about finding a
way to live that satisfies more of your deeper needs—needs you
might not even have realized you have because you have been so
caught up in listening to what your TV tells you are the needs
you *ought* to have. (Advertisers depend on emulative
consumption.)

The downshifting process, if you do it properly, is not just a
physical, practical process. It's an emotional process also.

We could use food as an analogy here. A plate of mashed
potato is nutritious but rather boring to eat. A plate of fries is
gratifying to the taste-buds but highly calorific and full of trans-
fats. However, an organically-grown potato baked in its jacket in
a wood fire, cut in half, sprinkled with grated cheese and lightly
broiled is not only delicious but nutritious as well. Downshifting
is not about making your life less tasty. It's about making your
life *more tasty and yet more wholesome at the same time*. The secret
of achieving that is to look carefully at each facet of your life—
the clothes you wear, the food you eat, the work you do, the way
you move around, the company you keep, the place you live in,
the lifestyle you follow, the things you buy, your leisure activities
and so on—in terms of (a) how well they serve your deepest
needs, (b) how well they fit with the needs of the Earth and (c)
how 'tasty' they are for you, personally.

So what are your deepest needs? Abraham Maslow—the
psychologist I mentioned in the previous chapter— pointed out
that our needs can be seen as a pyramid. The base level needs are
for survival, which means food, water, fresh air etc. The next
level needs are the 'safety' needs, such as a feeling of security,
having enough money to live on, a roof over one's head. Then

come the 'love and belonging' needs—our need for family, friends and lovers—the 'esteem' needs such as confidence and respect, and finally the need for 'self-actualization' or becoming all that we can potentially be.

The advertising industry manipulates us in such a way that we start half-believing it is the plasma screen TV, the latest model car and the designer clothes we need, whereas in fact what we really need is to feel comfortable, safe, secure, loved, worthwhile and happy in ourselves. We might imagine that our self-esteem rests on the image we present to the world. In fact, all of us have built-in sensors that tell us whether we like, admire or respect another person and it really has nothing to do with that person's wristwatch or car or fancy furniture. It has to do with what I call their authentic 'essence'—i.e. who they really are underneath. No matter how good the window-dressing is, we don't buy from a store unless we like the quality of the goods inside. And it is just the same with people.

At the same time, we all have a sense of the aesthetic. We like to present well, to be fit and healthy and attractive. We enjoy good-quality things around us. And we love to play, to have fun. So downshifting does not mean that we have to be dowdy or look scruffy. It does not mean that we cannot enjoy a bottle of good wine or dress up for a party. Downshifters do not necessarily have to eat crunchy granola and the wearing of Birkenstocks is definitely not mandatory. (Even though they *are* the comfiest sandals ever!)

So one of the aims of downshifting is to make ourselves happier, more contented, more peaceful, more satisfied with our lives. And to bring much more delight into our days. In order to do that, we have to wake up to all the unnecessary pressures to which we have been subjected and work out, skillfully, how to ease our way out from under these and achieve a more restful, better balanced and more deeply satisfying way to live which does not 'cost the Earth'.

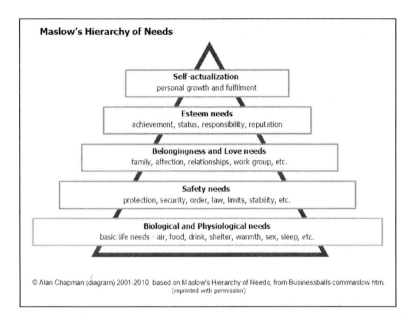

Maslow's Hierarchy of Needs

Self-actualization
personal growth and fulfilment

Esteem needs
achievement, status, responsibility, reputation

Belongingness and Love needs
family, affection, relationships, work group, etc.

Safety needs
protection, security, order, law, limits, stability, etc.

Biological and Physiological needs
basic life needs - air, food, drink, shelter, warmth, sex, sleep, etc.

© Alan Chapman (diagram) 2001-2010, based on Maslow's Hierarchy of Needs, from Businessballs.com/maslow.htm.
(reprinted with permission)

Why is downshifting spiritual as well as practical?

It is in that topmost tip of Maslow's pyramid that what we think of as the psychological and emotional parts of ourselves begin imperceptibly to blend into what we call the spiritual aspects.

When, as a graduate student in psychology, I began to study the psychology of the East and compare it with that of the West I was astonished, at first, to discover that in Eastern thought there was never a distinction between psychology and spirituality. They have always been part of the same thing. When someone came to the Buddha with a problem, the prescription for resolving the problem would usually be a spiritual one. A person worried about death, for example, would be instructed to sit in a graveyard and meditate on the whole notion of impermanence. But in recent times, as science began to dominate our thinking, medicine began to expand its sphere of activity to take in the mind as well as the body. Then it began, unfortunately, to brainwash us into believing that the mind and body are separate, which of course they are really not. So we in the West have been fooled into believing that there is a gap between psychology and spirituality when in fact there is none.

We have also, because of the power of institutionalized religion, confused spirituality with religion, whereas they are not the same thing at all. Certainly it is true that for many millions of people, spirituality is expressed through some form of religion, just as creativity may be expressed through some form of art. But creativity is not limited to art. Creativity can also be expressed by play, by writing, by cooking, by architecture, by creating fancy dress costumes, organizing a party or preparing a picnic. Likewise, our spirituality—which, like creativity, is something we all possess—is by no means limited to religion. It can show itself in any one of a million ways.

In a practical sense, the process of downshifting almost always involves some kind of stripping away. We go through our wardrobes, our attics, our garages; we cart things to the recycling depot or advertise them on Freecycle, and we donate to charity all the books and clothing and household goods that we no longer need. We divest ourselves of clutter so that we can move more freely and lightly through life.

Likewise, we go through the emotional attics and basements of our lives and declutter them too. We stop doing things we no longer enjoy. We divest ourselves of outworn obligations, allow the outworn relationships (those so-called 'friendships' that really aren't) to dwindle and re-examine our priorities to see how we would rather spend our time and energy and with whom.

Inevitably, as we move further into these processes, we shall eventually notice that there is also a stripping away of another kind. Just as the dust and grime of years can dull the face of a painting, years of overwork and enslavement to the culture of consumerism and the mainstream media can cover our own spiritual faces. When we downshift and all those are gradually stripped away, we start to come face to face with what we really value, what we really believe. As one of my spiritual teachers used to ask, "What is your life consecrated to?" If your life is consecrated to making and spending money, keeping up with the Joneses, filling every minute of your waking day with work or TV, meaningless socializing and endlessly exchanging text messages, there is very little opportunity to become aware of the deeper levels of who you really are. When you downshift, even if you do it initially to make yourself happier and healthier, your life inevitably becomes consecrated, in the end, not just to your own happiness but to the happiness and health of the whole planet. Because the more deeply you look into what downshifting is really about, the sooner you will discover the oldest and most sacred piece of wisdom that exists. Which is that there really is no separation between us and the Earth on which we walk. Every molecule, every atom of everything that is here in our world has been here since the beginning —apart from a few meteors and bits of space dust that have landed more recently. It is all part of what was once a giant fireball that cooled and became a planet and upon whose surface water formed from gas, and plants and animals emerged from the water. The stuff of which we are made is not new. It is merely recycled. Matter doesn't come from somewhere else. It just recycles endlessly. We *are* the planet and the planet is us. Whatever we do to the planet we do to ourselves, and vice versa.

And that is as spiritual as it can possibly get.

The problem is that we humans, through our science and technology, are the first species that ever had enough power to change the climate itself, to extract all the fossil fuels from the ground and pollute everything so badly that the survival of most living species—and certainly our own—is now in jeopardy.

The Earth will survive, come what may, even if it ends up as barren rock and desert, like the moon or Mars. But if we love our children and our grandchildren, if we love the beauty of Nature and all its wonderful diversity, then doing our part to preserve and protect these fragile things becomes not just a personal choice but a sacred duty. That's the spiritual part of 'why?'

Chapter 3

The 'when?' questions

When should you take the first step?

So when to start? Well my first answer may surprise you. If you have bought this book or borrowed it from the library—or even picked it up from somewhere and read it as far as this point— then in fact you have already started. Like many processes in our lives, downshifting begins with attention, moves from attention to *in*tention and then from intention to commission.

What prompted you to open this book? Something you read or heard, something that someone said to you or even something that arose from the depths of your own unconscious mind and thrust itself into your waking consciousness will have caused you to start paying attention to the idea of downshifting. Since we are all connected, there are often movements that happen deep within what Carl Jung called the Collective Unconscious which, like deep ocean currents, affect what is happening on the surface at many different places at once. So when ideas arise in us spontaneously we often find that similar ideas have arisen in the same way in other people at roughly the same time. It seems like a coincidence, but it isn't really. It only looks like that because we forget about the connection thing (remember those experiments with the paired particles that I mentioned in Chapter 1?). The idea of downshifting is one such ocean current that is moving through our Western culture at this time, even though its effects are not all that visible on the surface of things at the moment. Unless you happen to be watching for them, like I do. In which case, you start noticing the little ripples every-where. And they are happening more and more. Not a tsunami yet, but eventually it will be. Because we all want to survive. And greening the world is the only way, now, that we can do that. No more kidding ourselves that someone will come up with a high-tech solution and all our problems will be magically fixed. In fact it is our technology that has enabled us to create this much mess. So the technology we need to be working on—e.g. smarter ways of using the power of the sun and the wind and the tides to create electricity—is vitally important but we must not expect that it will enable us to go on living the way we are now because electricity is only one piece of the solution. We must all work on assembling the other pieces.

For you, the downshifting process is already well under way. The chances are, if you have read this far, that you have already moved from the attention phase to the edge of the intention phase. Or you may have formulated the intention in your mind and you are about to move into the final phase—commission. In other words, you thought about it, you decided to do it, you even know, more or less, why you want to do it and all that remains now is to figure out what exactly to do and how this is going to happen. But there is more to be said about the 'when'.

...but when is the right time for you?

As I pointed out earlier, you have in fact already started the process because you are reading this book and you have begun to consider what practical moves you might take. You are ready to take the next step. So when should you do that? This time, 'now' is not necessarily the right answer. That is because the optimum time to embark on a project of any kind or to move into a new phase of your life is when it *feels right on all counts*.

Eric Berne, the famous psychologist and author of the seminal book *Games People Play*,[7] popularized a way of looking at human nature that proved to be one of the best psychotherapy tools ever invented. It is as though the human psyche is not a unitary thing but a trinity of 3 psyches: the Parent, the Adult and the Child. One of the functions of our Parent self is to be an emotional filing cabinet for all the 'oughts' and 'shoulds' and 'dos' and 'don'ts' and rules and recipes we have learned throughout our lives and chosen to retain. The Parent self is a complex creature. Like all parents it can be both nurturing and strict, disapproving or kind. Our Adult self is simpler. Like a computer, it merely computes. In other words, it reasons, plans, solves problems, stores knowledge (in a dispassionate way) and figures things out.

The Child self is also complex. By nature it is free, joyful, pleasure-seeking, curious and uninhibited. But experience— especially painful experience or neglect at an early age—can maim and stunt it and render it fearful, timid and lacking in trust.

So the right answer to the question about the right time to downshift—or in fact the right time to do anything—is this. The right time is of course when the opportunity arises. But even if the opportunity is there, it is not time to take it unless and until:

> your inner Parent approves of it
>
> your inner Child is excited about it, and
>
> your Adult has taken the other two voices into consideration and has decided what to do and how and when and where and why you should do it.

Chapter 4

The 'how?' questions

How do you actually go about it?

Let's look again at that concept of 'joining the dots'.

The key to answering the 'how?' question is to keep in mind at every single moment that whatever we do affects the world around us in some way or another. I am a sucker for detective stories and one thing I have learned from reading them is that everywhere you go you leave traces of yourself—skin cells, tiny fibers, whatever. The air we breathe in is the air some other organism breathed out. Remember the so-called 'butterfly effect'? It is a term in modern physics and Wikipedia defines it thus:

> The phrase refers to the idea that a butterfly's wings might create tiny changes in the atmosphere that may ultimately alter the path of a tornado or delay, accelerate or even prevent the occurrence of a tornado in a certain location. ...While the butterfly does not "cause" the tornado in the sense of providing the energy for the tornado, it does "cause" it in the sense that the flap of its wings is an essential part of the initial conditions resulting in a tornado, and without that flap that particular tornado would not have existed.

Even the tiniest action we take can influence events at a distance. And this is what dot-joining is all about. So our task is to be ever-mindful of this principle.

Dot-joining is particularly potent principle when a number of people are doing it together. Example: I might say to myself, "*Oh I may as well book that flight because even if I don't, the plane will go anyway so what difference does it make?"* Probably not a lot in that particular instance. But the more people who decide not to fly, the emptier the planes will be. And airline companies don't like empty seats. (Have you noticed how almost every flight these days seems to be jam-packed? Not like in the old days when, if you were lucky, you could stretch out over three seats and have a good nap.) So over time, the more empty seats there are, the more cuts to the schedule there will soon be and the fewer planes will be in the air. Which means less oil being used up and less pollution up in the higher levels of the atmosphere where it does so much more damage than at ground level.

Downshifting means thinking about these things for yourself rather than expecting to be reminded. Governments won't set the example because they fear loss of popularity, and corporations won't because they rely on profits. We have to take the lead so that eventually they follow.

The newspapers and radio and TV programs are not going to join the dots for us because their existence depends on our continuing to buy stuff from the companies whose advertising keeps them in business. We have to do our own dot-joining. Unfortunately lots of people are slow to grasp the connection between the way we live our individual lives and the problems we as a species are collectively facing. The market forces driving our consumer society are so strong and all-pervasive that it takes an enormous amount of effort to resist and defy them. When I wrote about this in my blog, one person commented that, " ...it's like swimming against Niagara Falls to Do The Right Thing." Yes, that's just how it feels sometimes. So we have to give a tremendous amount of deliberate thought to the ways in which our own behavior, our own lifestyles and all the small choices we make, day by day, affect what is happening in the wider world. Where does our rubbish end up? How much carbon are we putting into the air when we take that bargain flight? When we swallow antibiotics and hormone pills and various other pharmaceutical products and some of that is excreted and goes down the drain, what effect might that have on the watercourses and the creatures that live in them? When we buy those cheap, chemical-sprayed supermarket bananas or that cheap, sweatshop-made T-shirt, whose life are we helping to damage in some other part of the world? How long before the plastic toys we bought for the kids' Christmas stockings end up in the landfill and how many centuries will it be before they break down—if ever? How much fossil fuel did it take to make that new, shiny gadget that we didn't really need and have managed for forty years without? (And on and on ....)

No TV commercials are ever going to remind us of these questions. They are geared to our forgetting, not to our remembering. The headwind of commerce blows relent-lessly, day in and day out. Buy, buy, buy. Spend, spend, spend. Use, use, use. Pushing against it takes effort and persistence. What we need to get through our heads is the fact that dozens of the small decisions we make, every day, do make a difference. Each decision, even if it is as tiny a decision as turning off a light switch, either adds to the problem or helps to ameliorate it.

Our national and global economic systems are all based on a growth model rather than a sustainability model. And since every one of us is part of both a national and a global economic system, the systems need us to keep consuming so that the growth can continue. Even though, like cancer, it is growth that's slowly killing us. The trouble is, if too many of us were to jump off our consumer treadmills, profits would go down. The companies would start laying off their workers. The workers would complain—and of course the workers are us, our partners, our children, our relatives, our friends ... As the comic strip character Pogo once so famously—and wisely— said, 'I have met the enemy, and it is us.'

Most loggers don't personally want to chop down the rainforest; they just want to keep their jobs in order to feed their families. Fishermen have absolutely no desire or intention to reduce the world's fish populations to zero, they just need to keep catching fish in order to survive. People who work in offices and stores and on factory floors all want to keep their jobs too. So round and around it goes and life on Earth keeps heading towards catastrophe. Even if it is not your job that would be at risk if everybody stopped buying what they didn't really need, it might be your father's or your daughter-in-law's or your cousin's. And even if nobody you know would be affected (which is highly unlikely), somebody would, somewhere. Lots of somebodies. The farmer in Kenya who, ten years ago, stopped producing vegetables to feed his family (plus a bit more to sell in the market) and switched to producing flowers for export so he could afford to send his kids to school needs me to keep on buying his carnations or his green beans or his cocoa. If I don't, his kids will starve because they can't eat flowers. We are all tangled in this together. So however can we possibly unpick it?

The answer is that we unpick it slowly, carefully, one little piece at a time. The first step is to start setting up parallel, alternative systems and supporting the alternative systems that already exist. Here's a list of practical, downshifting actions both large and small. Pick a couple to get started:

Dig up the lawn and grow veggies, just like we did in World War Two. (Or grow things in containers.)

Stay out of supermarkets and support local stores whenever and wherever you can find them.

Patronize farmers' markets and CSAs (community supported agriculture schemes) and local box schemes.

Join a co-op.

Switch to green energy suppliers.

Install a solar water heater.

Install a wind turbine.

Insulate your house more effectively.

Lower the thermostat a degree or three.

Compost your waste.

Start a worm farm.

If you live in the country, consider building a composting toilet.

Leave your car at home whenever you can and use public transport or walk or ride a bike. Or at least carpool or consider sharing car ownership with other families like they do in Germany.

Dry your washing in the sun and wind.

Borrow books and videos from the library instead of buying them.

Sign up to the 'compact' (challenge yourself to buy nothing for a year except food and other necessities).

Fly as little as you possibly can.

Make your own gifts or give food items that will be consumed

Switch off lights and appliances when not in use.

Reduce, repair, re-use, recycle, declutter, downsize ....

When we learn to differentiate between our needs and our wants, we can get sober (i.e. heal from our addiction to unnecessary stuff). We can stop being 'users' of consumerism's drugs. How could you reduce your needs so that you could spend more time with your family or in doing the things you love? How could you be fitter, healthier, more active, more creative?

Maybe we can also stop being dealers in consumerism's drugs, too. Think about your work: is it what the Buddha called 'Right Livelihood'? If not, would it be possible to use your skills in something more benign and better for the planet and still earn enough money to survive on?

Like relay runners, the two systems need to run side by side until the new one can take over completely. Slowly, gradually, we are setting up alternative systems and at present these are running parallel with the mainstream ones. Little by little, the alternative systems are getting bigger and stronger. Compared to the vast system they are intended eventually to replace, they seem almost laughably tiny. Like a mosquito trying to replace an elephant. Yet on every graph you look at, they are growing. There are heaps more farmers' markets than there were ten years ago, lots more veg box schemes and 'made locally' labels, more LETS schemes, more towns climbing on the 'transition town' bandwagon, more people working from home, more wind farms, more solar panels, more hybrid cars, more recycling schemes, more intelligent minds turning to research in alternative technology, more businesses trying to 'out-green' each other, and more and more people turning green.

When I was born, plastic had not yet been invented. In my first school, we wrote with pencils or with nib pens dipped in ink and there were no such things as ballpoints yet. Nobody I knew had a refrigerator and many households had no telephone. When I was in high school there was no TV, no PCs, no Internet, no mobile phones, no iPods, no fax machines, no jumbo jets, no microwave ovens. A lot can change in a short time. We need big changes now, and as fast as possible. So how can we bring them about? Well firstly, by doing as Gandhi exhorted us to do and being the change we want to see. And secondly by visualizing a green world. The more people who visualize it, the sooner it can come to pass, for thoughts have energy.

See the change, be the change. Those are our twin tasks. This may be a mosquito-sized movement now, but, as Gandhi also pointed out, if you think a mosquito is too small to matter, you've never had one in your tent.

How do you overcome your doubts and fears?
When we make a decision to create radical changes in our lives, there are two kinds of stumbling blocks it is useful to anticipate. If we anticipate them we can also anticipate how we might deal with them if and when they loom up in our path. As the saying

goes, 'forewarned is forearmed.'

Both kinds of stumbling blocks have to do with the arising of doubts and fears.

The first of these—though not necessarily the first to arise—is our own set of doubts and fears. How these might manifest, and in fact whether they manifest at all, depends to a great extent on what sort of people we are. Are you a worrier? If so, a couple of weeks after you have announced that you are planning to downshift you might find yourself suddenly waking in the middle of the night thinking, '*Oh hell, what am I doing? What if....?*' And for worriers (I know this because I'm one myself), doubts and fears that arise in the middle of the night are like a bunch of escaped lions running rampant. With no bars of rationality to hold them in and with the calm, experienced zookeeper of my daytime mind not around to subdue them with the anesthetic darts of common sense and optimism, they can easily render me helpless and keep me sleepless for hours. If you have actually started the downshifting process in a radical way, such as resigning from a full-time job, putting your five-bedroomed house on the market or selling one of your cars, the danger is of course exacerbated.

Or are you a Pollyanna? Some people who appear to be 100% positive and optimistic at all times really are like that through and through. Nothing ever seems to worry them. They take life lightly and contentedly and when problems arise they remain unruffled and deal with them swiftly and competently. Lucky people! The Pollyannas I mostly encounter, however, are folks who resolutely suppress any doubts or fears they may have in order to present a positive face to the world. They may not even realize they have any doubts or fears, in which case they are not *sup*pressing them but *re*pressing them (in other words, they are doing it unconsciously). There's a simple way of knowing whether or not this applies to you. If someone close to you expresses his or her own doubts or fears about your downshifting plans do you find yourself jumping in and vigorously opposing that person's arguments, rather than listening with a totally calm and open mind? (And as you do that, are you maybe feeling a knot of discomfort around your solar plexus somewhere?) If you answered '*yes*', you are probably repressing doubts and fears of your own.

If you find this happening, here's the magic solution:

Listen completely to what the other person is saying and put yourself completely in his or her place. Own those doubts and fears as if they were your own. Because they probably are. And once they are owned and accepted and brought out into the light, they can be dealt with. Having doubts or fears about a project doesn't mean you can't or won't go through with it, any more than fearing the dentist means letting your teeth rot. It is normal to have doubts and be fearful about any kind of change in our lives, whether positive or negative. Think of all those brides that get the pre-wedding jitters or the actors shivering in the wings with stage fright. The wedding still happens; the show still goes on; the tooth gets filled. We survive and we thrive. (It's called *life*!)

Even if you are neither a worrier or a Pollyanna with a tummyful of repressed or suppressed fears and doubts, you still might find that some arise. They could be triggered by circumstances. You put your house on the market a month ago, nobody has come to inspect it yet and you just read this morning that the housing market is starting another slump. Your boss gave you permission to telecommute and come into the office just one day a month, so you decided to move house and get a bicycle but now there's been an unexpected re-shuffle at top management level and the new CEO is known to disapprove of employees working from home. Oops!

Obviously I can't tell you how to deal with the problems themselves, since that would take umpteen more volumes covering every possible circumstance. But I can share the problem-solving formula that works best for me in pretty much any circumstance.

Step 1.

Figure out who owns the problem. If the answer is 'I do' proceed to Step 2.

Step 2.

Decide whether I own it fully or whether the ownership is shared. If the latter, proceed to Step 3. (Otherwise go straight to Step 4.)

Step 3.

If the problem is a shared one, sit down and discuss the problem fully with the other person or people who share ownership of it. Then proceed *together* to Step 4.

Step 4.

Brainstorm. This means write down every possible solution anyone present can possibly think of, including the crazy, way out and illegal ones (especially the crazy, way out and illegal ones because just listing them helps to switch on your creativity, believe it or not. And because those are often good for a laugh and laughter relaxes tension.). *Don't evaluate any solutions at this stage.* Not even a little bit. Just list everything you can think of. When you are totally done, proceed to Step 5.

Step 5.

Go through the longlist, evaluating it as you go and crossing things off till you end up with a workable shortlist. Repeat this process several times if necessary, looking at all the pros and cons—if necessary, adding up the pros and cons and comparing them—until your solution becomes really clear or there is a tie between two options. Be sure to take intuition, gut feelings etc into account though. Some solutions *feel* more right than others, even if the numbers don't stack up quite as well. Remember to consult your inner Child and your inner Parent, as explained in Chapter 3, so that your Adult can factor these in. In the case of a tie, figure out whether there might be a composite solution (combining the best bits of each) or whether a compromise is needed. Or maybe a vote. Ideally, let some time elapse before a final decision is made so that you can sleep on it, notice what comes up in your dreams and daydreams, examine any further doubts or ideas that pop up. Consensus tends usually to be a slow and laborious process, whether it is consensus between individuals in a group or an inner consensus between the various aspects of your psyche. But decisions reached by consensus are usually easier to stick to and everyone's commitment to them is usually high.

Step 6.

Make sure that you (and the others, if this involves anyone else) (a) are totally clear on how the solution is going to be implemented and (b) have worked out how the results are going to be evaluated and when and by whom.

The second stumbling block you may encounter when you decide to downshift is the doubts and fears of others. Obviously, this is an even more significant factor when you are part of a family. In which case, any decision about major changes has to be agreed by your partner and everyone has to feel OK about it. It can get tricky when there are children involved. Leaving friends, changing schools, leaving a neighborhood, having to share a bedroom—these can all be huge issues for a child, and the older the child, the bigger those issues are. My own family was forced to relocate unexpectedly when I was 15 and I still remember what hell I went through in those next few months. So it is important to take everyone's feelings and needs into account and to deal kindly and carefully with all doubts and fears expressed by all members. We all need to feel valued and respected. And when we are young and powerless and our parents ride roughshod over our feelings it makes us feel un-valued, un-respected and in many cases resentful. That sort of thing can leave lifelong scars.

Remember, there are many smaller, less problematical elements of downshifting that can be introduced into family life without causing any trauma at all. Things like cooking from scratch, taking holidays nearer home, insulating the walls and the loft, growing some of your own food, buying local produce, turning the thermostat down a notch...and so on. Maybe it is better to stick with those for now and leave any major, potentially disruptive ones till the kids leave for college.

Other people pouring cold water on your ideas, laughing at your idealism, telling you that you are wasting your time and so on can be a real downer. I have found that in situations like that it is better to walk away than to argue. *"I have my ideas and you have yours. Let's both respect our differences and change the subject shall we?"* is a good comeback. Listening to disparaging comments from others means that you are at risk of absorbing their negativity, which is only going to weaken your energy. Opposing people and arguing with them rarely convinces them. It's far more likely to drive them further into their own corner. It energizes them. You don't have to argue your case. Just follow Gandhi's famous maxim and simply be the change you want to see happen in the world, rather than arguing for it. That is what works.

How does this mesh with your beliefs or religion?

One big one for some people might be *"How does the philosophy of downshifting accord with my spiritual and/or religious beliefs?"* There are a few people (though I very much doubt that any of them will be reading this book) who believe that trashing the planet is a Good Thing because it is all part of a divine plan, speeding the movement towards a final judgment day when all the good guys will be fast-tracked into heaven and the baddies will stay down here and perish as the whole thing goes up in smoke. I kid you not. There *are* people who really believe that! They call themselves Christians but there is no way Jesus Christ would ever have condoned such a horrible attitude. There are many indications that he was a greenie himself.[8] Most Christians I know believe, nowadays, that we should be taking better care of the Earth than we are. They see it is as our duty to look after the garden we inherited so that we can pass it on in good condition to the generations who come after us. So living more simply, conserving resources and being green is totally compatible with all types of Christianity that truly are based on the teachings of Christ who as we know lived an utterly simple life. So downshifting is a very Christian process, there is a growing trend towards green activism in the churches and I've noticed the same thing in other religions, also, over recent years.

One might expect that in any religious tradition, the more emphasis there is on some sort of heaven or paradise after death, the less concern there is about the Earth. And to a certain extent I think that is true. Yet if it were the only deciding factor, we would logically expect all pagans to be the greenest and most Earth-respecting and simple-living folk on the planet and that is not always the case. The last photo I saw of Stonehenge the morning after a crowd of thousands had celebrated the solstice sunrise, I was appalled at the mess of trash they left behind.

So to answer, myself, the question I posed at the outset: I think that true love and respect for the Earth, awareness of one's place in it—and duty towards it—is independent of any allegiance to or membership of a formal religious or spiritual tradition or organization. It is an individual thing.

I also believe that greenness, simple living and Earth-care are all 100% compatible with all the religious and spiritual traditions.

Greenness, simple living and Earth-care are not just practical aspects of our lives. They are spiritual actions, spiritual statements in their own right. In the pursuit of these goals, our spirits will be satisfied in a deeper, richer way than they have ever been before. This is partly because as we move away from materialism and consumerism and into deeper relationship and harmony with the Earth and with Nature, we are also creating a deeper harmony within ourselves, for we ourselves, as I pointed out earlier, are as much a part of Nature as a leaf on a tree or a bird on a branch. Also because many of the simple pleasures and activities that downshifters get into, such as exchanging hand-made gifts, eating meals together, walking and cycling instead of driving, getting involved with our local communities, growing food in our gardens or hanging our washing to dry in the sun and breeze are intrinsically satisfying. They bring more pleasure to our senses. And because they are all, in one way or another, more interactive, they better suit our natures, for humans are relational beings. To be physically and emotionally healthy, we not only need to be active, we need a certain level of *inter*action, not only with each other but with other creatures, with the soil, the sunshine and the trees. If that were not so, why do you suppose solitary confinement is one of the sternest punishments we can mete out for criminal behavior?

I have also discovered that living simply, which usually means doing more things for ourselves and relying less on machines and factory workers to do them for us, not only gives us a bit more physical exercise, which is good for us, but it also gives us more time to think and contemplate. I noticed many years ago that some of my best ideas come to me when I'm gardening or when I'm out walking. Also when I'm showering or swimming or hand-washing clothes and pegging them on the line. Physical activity, movement and running water all seem to nourish our creativity. Have you noticed how people, when they have a tough problem to solve, often instinctively pace up and down? It is at these times, too, that some of the best spiritual insights seem to appear, suddenly, in the foreground of the mind.

So to put it really simply, I believe that downshifting is conducive to spiritual deepening. That has been my own experience, anyway. I hope it comes true for you also.

Chapter 5

The 'where?' questions

Do you need to move house?

I have noticed that a lot of people seem to equate downshifting with selling one's house in the city or suburbs, moving to a few acres in the country, setting up solar panels or a windmill, catching rainwater, keeping chickens and spending an inordinate amount of time sloshing around in the mud.

Some of the people who talk to me about that do so with a wistful look in their eyes. They have always had a dream, they tell me, of 'going back to the land', living 'closer to Nature' (as though any of us could live any closer to Nature than being part of it, which we all inescapably are, given that we are an animal species!), growing their own food, yadda yadda... It is amazing how prevalent this romantic vision of self-sufficiency is. And some people do achieve it. Not only do they achieve it but they enjoy it. However, the back-to-the-land trip can be a very bumpy ride and it most certainly is not for everyone.

There are other people who also believe that back-to-the-land is synonymous with downshifting but rather than looking wistful they shudder at the thought of it. Swapping one's pinstripe suit for a pair of overalls and embarking on a life of bucolic self-sufficiency is a huge challenge and it takes a certain kind of person to do it. So if you are not that sort of person it would be stupid to try. Remember that famous motto carved over the doorway in ancient Delphi? 'Know Thyself', it said—a piece of advice that has never been bettered. Get to know yourself, your likes and dislikes, your capabilities, your strengths and weaknesses, talents, skills and ambitions. Think about what you are best at and what you don't do so well. Be totally honest with yourself. Having limitations does not mean that you are not OK. We all have limitations. There is nobody who is good at everything. Be who you are and try to get really comfortable with that. Not as an excuse for not doing what needs to be done but as a means to work out how best to do it. That way, you can craft a life that really works for you, one that is custom-made to suit your personality and preferences.

So rather than aspiring to some romantic dream of what you think downshifting ought to look like, it is really important to start with who you are—and who your family members are too, if you are part of a family—and what style of downshifting would suit *you* the best.

Believing that downshifting means back-to-the-land but not wanting to live in the country can provide an all-too-convenient excuse for doing nothing. But the truth is that there are many ways of downshifting and the crucial task that faces you is how to tailor yours to fit *you* and *your* life. Yes, you do have a responsibility to do something. We all have. Because we are all in this together and unless every single one of us does his or her bit the result will be disaster. But you need not follow anyone else's recipe. You simply have to work out where your particular efforts will be best directed. That is your personal 'where' question and you are the only one who can answer it.

My partner and I do live in the country, although our garden is too small to supply all the fruit and veggies we need and we don't have to keep chickens because our neighbor keeps lots and is happy to sell us eggs. But in the last quarter-century we have also lived in the suburbs, in an inner-city townhouse, a downtown apartment, a commune (briefly) and on 30 acres in the Australian bush. In every one of those settings we have success-fully managed to keep our carbon output to the minimum, our eco-footprint way below the national average and our lifestyles as green as grass. You may be surprised to learn that during the Australian bush phase, which was pure back-to-the-landsville, complete with composting toilet, mud bricks and rainwater, our footprint was actually higher than during any of the other phases. Why? Because turning 30 acres of bush into a human habitation uses up a huge amount of raw materials. We needed rainwater tanks, hundreds of yards of polypipe to bring water from the stream up to the veggie garden, solar panels, deep cell batteries, an inverter, a back-up generator (and fuel to run it), wire netting to keep the wallabies out of the cabbages, fencing to keep out the neighbor's sheep. Plus the fact that living in an isolated place like that meant having and running a vehicle—of necessity a heavy 4WD one—and a trailer and all the fuel needed to drive to the nearest human settlement for supplies. Whereas in the city we could live without a car, do our shopping on foot or by bicycle and use public transport to visit our friends and family. Our small, terrace house stayed warm because of the insulating effect of the houses either side, which meant lower heating bills, yet we could still grow some things in the garden and compost our waste. And we had curbside recycling. In the bush there was no recycling except that which we did ourselves (e.g. using all the old newspapers and other paper waste as mulch in the garden) and non-recyclable rubbish had to be carried several miles to the tip by car.

So the practical answer to the 'where' questions are very short and simple. Where do you start? You start from where you are. Where do you live? You live wherever you want to live, wherever you are happy, wherever you can afford to live and you start from that.

Where do you feel most at home?

'Where' becomes a literal, geographical question only if you are considering moving to a different house or area. If you think downshifting for you is going to involve a physical move, think very carefully before you decide to do it. My reasons for saying that are scattered throughout the book so I won't go into them specifically here. But if moving to another part of the country or abroad is a real option for you, I would advise you to do a lot of research into it first and talk to as many people as you can find who have done what you are thinking of doing.

Whole books have been written on our relationship to place (and I could probably write one myself as this has been a big factor in my own life). Some species, like the albatross, the salmon or the gray whale, range over thousands of miles; some, like the thrush who sings in the sycamore tree by our house, never move more than a mile from where they were born. Likewise, some humans are by nature nomads and love to wander, whereas others are, whether they know it or not, deeply connected to territory. And there are others who, although they can bond to places, are also adaptable. Like cats, they may be uncomfortable at first but after a while they adapt. Before you decide to move your territory, be sure you know which category you fall into and plan accordingly.

There is another important question to ask in the 'where' category and that is 'where do I turn for guidance/inspiration/information/support?

Downshifting is, to be sure, a growing trend, not just in our own country but right across the world. Nevertheless, the way that most people get to know what is going on in the world is by reading newspapers and watching television. And unfortunately all the major newspapers and television stations are owned by powerful corporations. For powerful corporations, profit is of paramount importance. Much of the profit comes from advertising. And advertising is about buying stuff. So anyone who relies for news and opinions on what is put forward by the mainstream media is being brainwashed daily (and I do not consider 'brainwashing' to be too strong a word for it) by the forces of materialism and consumerism.

However, thanks to the power of the Internet, it is possible, nowadays, to find alternative news sources elsewhere, such as in the 'blogosphere'. I have not had a TV set in the house since 1985 and I have a wonderful feeling of lightness and wellbeing that comes from being to a great extent free of the pressures and preoccupations of mainstream culture. I am not saying that you should get rid of your TV set. But I do at least urge you to:

keep it switched off unless you are actually watching it

choose carefully, in advance, what programs you will watch, and stick to those, rather than channel-surfing

limit children to no more than an hour and a half of total 'screen time' per day (that includes electronic games and leisure activities on the computer)

mute all commercials

either keep the TV set in a cabinet or cover it with a throw when it is not being watched so that it does not become the central point of focus for the room it's in. (There is a subliminal message in TV sets being the point to which the eye is always drawn.)

I also urge you to seek out alternative news sources, subscribe to blogs like Huffington Post, join social networks and discussion groups that are focused around green issues and simple living (for example there are lots of green groups on Facebook and umpteen green blogs and websites listed on Technorati) and seek out companions, neighbors and colleagues who share your ideas. Some people thrive on being 'different'. But for many others, as I have mentioned elsewhere in the book, it is hard to find oneself constantly part of a minority group. It's hard to be the lone voice speaking up for vegetarianism in a group of carnivores, for paganism in a group of traditional Christians, for restraint in a group of climate change scoffers, for downshifting in a group of get-ahead materialists or for spiritual values in a group of cynical atheists. For many it is a constant, wearying struggle always to be swimming against the tide. So seek out your own kind.

Nurture friendships with other downshifters. Join—or start—a downshifting group. Cecile Andrews has a whole lot about how to do that in her book on simplicity circles.[9] Flock with birds of your feather.[10] These are some of the ways you will unhook yourself from the culture of emulative consumption. Eventually you will reach a point where you are so unhooked that many of the things others yearn for you will find ugly, distasteful or even obscene. Your values will have undergone a sea change.

Above all, believe in yourself and in your own authority. You know better than anyone else on Earth what is best for you. So ignore the detractors and cynics. Go for it.

Where do you get your inspiration and guidance?

We need to ask ourselves from where we get inspiration, encouragement and guidance to keep us going along what can sometimes be a lonely and difficult path.

Nowadays, since issues like climate change and peak oil became a mainstream talking point, some religious leaders are now exhorting their congregations to do more towards caring for the planet and to downshift to more environmentally conscious lifestyles. Sad to say, a lot of the blame for the pickle our planet is in can be placed at the door of organized religion, with its historical attempts to prise humans out of their deep embeddedness in the natural world and interest them, instead, in promises of eternal life in some other dimension. But let's just be glad that the churches are finally starting to encourage greenness, even though their sermons, just like most secular sermons about 'the environment', are largely if not wholly motivated by self-interest. We must save the forests (so that we can breathe oxygen), protect the oceans (so that we can go on eating fish) conserve resources (so that we can eke out what's left of the oil), downshift (so that we don't all finish up starving to death because there are too many of us and not enough food to go round) and so on. It is always all about *us*. And sometimes, as an afterthought, the other species with whom we share the planet. After all, if we let them all die out, then we wouldn't have those fascinating nature programs to watch on TV any more, would we? (Oops, I am sounding cynical.)

Self-interest has always been a good motivator. But, as we have already discussed, it is not always easy to join the dots and to make connections between an action we take today and our wellbeing—or someone else's wellbeing—in the future, or even in the present.

The deepest, strongest and most meaningful and enduring motivation is the spiritual one. Put quite simply: we *are* the planet. What we do to Her, we do to ourselves. When we truly *love* the Earth we walk on, when we respect and have reverence for every other life form, when we really get it that every being has intrinsic value and everything is sacred, then everything else falls into place. That's when downshifting becomes as natural—and as vitally important to us—as breathing. In our love of Gaia, that is where we can find the inspiration and the guidance that we are seeking.

But it is all very well in theory.

It's easy to love the Earth on a bright and sunny morning and when things are going well. It's easy to love a fluffy kitten or a cute little wren, the perfection of a snowflake, the splendor of a rainbow over the mountains.

But can you feel equally kindly towards the sparrowhawk that swoops down and snatches the wren? Can you love a virus? Can you have reverence for an earthquake? A tsunami?

We know that the ideal is to love others—especially our partners and our children— unconditionally, but sometimes it is hard. How much harder to love a planet that as well as awesomely beautiful can also be awesomely destructive, unspeakably harsh. And despite how prettily the stars twinkle in the night sky, how much harder still it is to love the vast and measureless universe in which that planet floats. A universe in which our own significance shrinks to zero and one whose origins remain shrouded in a mystery that is utterly incomprehensible to our puny, human minds. Thinking about that can soon make us fearful and contracted.

At a psychic level most of us spend our whole lives in this contracted state. Fear makes us cautious. The lack of certainty terrifies us. The possibility of calamity narrows our vision. It makes us shrivel up, huddle into ourselves, vainly seeking comfort by curling up in a ball, like a hedgehog, rather than remaining fully open to everything that is around us and open to all the uncertainties of the next moment. Most of us are afraid, most of the time, though often not consciously so. We fear illness, we fear death, we fear the unknown future. The great mystery that is life scares most of us rigid. So we snuggle desperately into the familiar—into our relationships, our work, our routines, our library books and movies: always seeking comfort. I've heard it called existential angst. Just to be alive is scary if you let yourself really face life—and death—full-on. So most of us, most of the time, distract ourselves from existential angst and our deep-seated fear of the unknown and what might happen in our personal—or planetary—future. We attempt to insulate ourselves in any way we can think of. Like seeking certainty where there really is none by following, blindly, the precepts and prescriptions of off-the-peg belief systems. In the same way that we seal up cracks in our houses so that no cold draught may enter, we fill up all the spaces in our consciousness into which fear may possibly creep. Thus we go shopping for things we don't really need, put iPods in our ears, jabber and text on our cell phones, stay busy with our computers, our social lives, our work, the TV …anything to stop ourselves from thinking too hard about all the unknowns that scare us and all the question marks hanging over us as individuals and as members of what may well be a doomed species.

The truth is that no matter how much we try to kid ourselves, there are no guarantees, no escapes and no safe places. I think that is what Christ meant when he said, "The foxes have holes and the birds of the air have nests, but the Son of Man hath not where to lay His head," (Matthew 8:20). We humans are stuck with our existential dilemma: the dilemma of knowing enough to be scared but not enough to comforted. We cannot unravel the Great Mystery. All we can do is take a deep breath, step forward and say "yes" to it.

Saying "yes" to everything, including the possibility of annihilation and the loss of all that we hold dear, from robins to eagles to ourselves and to all illusions of security and certainty, is the only true course open to us. Opening up to whatever may happen, opening up to the unknown future, saying "yes" to life —*no matter what*—is, I believe, the ultimate spiritual challenge. It is every bit as difficult to do as striding confidently down an icy hill on a winter morning, looking up and out at the world instead of creeping along, staring anxiously down at one's boots. But only after we have accepted all the possibilities can we stride confidently into action. Only when we have faced the worst that might happen to us and to our world can we work tirelessly to create the peaceful, abundant, green world of which we dream. Courage is not about the denial of fear. It is about facing the fear and moving beyond it.

That is where we find our guidance, our inspiration and a wellspring of spiritual energy.

Chapter 6

The 'who?' questions

Who is downshifting and who needs to?

I've heard it said that that there are just two types of people: greenies who care about the planet and greedy consumers who don't. Other people believe that the two types are sensible people who just want to be left alone to get on with their lives and stupid hippies who sit in trees and live on welfare and bang on about climate change all the time. The way I see it, there are *six* types of people. These are:

(a) The people who care about the wellbeing of our planet and are trying their best to make sure it remains beautiful and green and habitable for future generations.

(b) The ones who care about the planet but haven't yet figured out the connections between that and the need to change their own lifestyles.

(c) The ones who care and who understand the connections but haven't made a start on changing anything yet, for whatever reason.

(d) The ones who care and who understand the connections but are so filled with despair that they have become cynical and have given up trying.

(e) The ones who really do care but have to stay in denial because their livelihood depends on pretending not to know and trying not to think about it.

(f) The ones who really don't know about any of this.

This book is for all six kinds. With any luck (and if it gets into their hands it probably *will* be by luck, so let's cross our fingers) the (f) group will finally wake up and realize what is going on around them and what they could start to do about it. Meanwhile:

> The (e) group (deniers) will start to close the gap between their private lives (where they dutifully recycle their trash and donate to environmental organizations that clean up oil spills), and their corporate lives where they help to make the decisions that cause the oil spills.
> The (d) group (cynics) will find themselves with some new hope.
> The (c) group (laggards) will be inspired to make a start.
> The puzzled (b)s will discover how they *can* make a difference after all.
> And those green and righteous (a)s will discover new ways to go even greener than they already are and donate this book to their local library when they have finished it.

Who are we and what is our role on the planet?

Downshifting is not merely a practical, economic action. And although the decision to declutter one's attic, work a shorter week, simplify one's life and embrace a gentler, more fulfilling way of being in the world is often primarily an emotional one, downshifting, as I've already suggested, is also a profoundly spiritual thing to do.

Whilst there are indications, particularly from the philosophy that has come down to us from certain indigenous peoples such as some of the Native American tribes, that earlier tribal peoples followed a spiritual path that was closely aligned with the laws and ways of Nature, most our modern versions of spirituality have jettisoned that sort of wisdom — at great cost.

Influential 19th Century philosophers encouraged the people of their times to believe that the role of human beings vis-à-vis the rest of Nature was to 'tame' it, to dissect it, dominate it and bend it to suit our own selfish needs. Or at least try to. This attitude gradually seeped through all the pores of our Western culture and now, as we watch the ice-caps melt, the fields lose fertility and resources shrink before our eyes, we are seeing that it was a dangerous mistake.

What we are finally, painfully realizing—perhaps too late or at best in the very nick of time—is that we are not separate beings who dwell *upon* the Earth, like insects crawling across the face of a pumpkin. We are an integral *part* of the Earth. Our bodies are made from Earth-stuff. The very atoms that make up our blood and bones and muscles have all been here since the Big Bang and will be here as long as the Earth exists.

When Darwin discovered that evolution proceeded to a great extent by the process of natural selection, he spoke of the 'survival of the fittest'. But the 'fittest' does not necessarily mean the biggest or toughest or most powerful. In fact, the organism with the best chance of survival for itself—and therefore for the survival of its DNA—is the one that *best fits* its particular niche in the ecosystem. For example, it is not the brawniest or most aggressive moth that escapes the bird's beak and thus is able to continue breeding, but the moth whose coloration blends in best with her immediate surroundings. Likewise, those individuals who learn to live green are the individuals best suited to a human future. Conscious downshifting, at this point in history, is a significant evolutionary step and those who are taking it will be the heroes of our descendants' history books.

Historians tell us that when the early humans lived as hunter-gatherers, they had enough to eat. For if there was no food around, they moved on until they found some. Once they discovered that the wild grasses could be cultivated for better yields and began to live in settlements instead, Nature, once seen as endlessly bountiful, began to be seen as capricious. For if, instead of moving to where the game is plentiful and there is food to gather, you live in one place and are dependent on what you can grow there, you are now at the mercy of the weather. If there is a prolonged drought, you may starve. Now, instead of trusting that there will always be enough, you fear that there won't. Insecurity is born. Instead of trusting the Earth to hold and nurture you, you imagine yourself subject to some unseen god who must be propitiated in order to keep the rain coming in the 'right' quantities and for the animals to breed and the crops to thrive. Instead of seeking out your food each day, like most other creatures, you begin to hoard in case of a bad season. Eventually, when civilization had become so complex that we could no longer keep track of the exchange of goods and services we needed to invent money. And then we began to hoard that. Instead of hoarding what we thought we might need or want, now we began hoarding the ability to buy it. And you know the rest of the story.

The point is, however, that there really is enough to go around. There always has been and if we make the right decisions now, there always can be. Though Earth's resources are finite, there has always been—and in fact still is—enough for all, but only if we are careful and everything is equitably and justly shared and nobody takes anyone else's share. This is the lesson of our times. This is the big challenge of our century: to rise above our basic natures and use the newer functions of our evolved brains to transcend those old impulses of greed and acquisitiveness born out of ancient fears and insecurities.

The planet's balance of needs and resources has held steady for millions of years. But we humans with our fear-induced greed and our mistaken sense of reality have begun to upset the balance. Fisherfolk, for example, have for thousands of years made their livelihood along the shores of the world's oceans. But our modern, rapacious methods of stripping those oceans have now created an unprecedented loss of fish. The once-teeming seas are nearly empty and fishermen's families are going hungry. This is just one example of the way we have unbalanced what was once a beautifully balanced system. There are other examples everywhere you look and I am sure you don't need me to list them. However, every single individual who downshifts to a simple, green lifestyle is shifting over from being part of the problem of planetary imbalance to being part of the solution.

Most people I know tell me they love Nature. But if we truly do love Nature, we must identify with it, honor its inbuilt laws and align our lifestyles, our emotions and our spiritual beliefs with the health and wellbeing of this gorgeous planet of which we are an integral part. For our fears and insecurities, our greed and the desire to hoard—all these, too, are part of who and what we are. They, too, are natural. They evolved with us. So, too, have these cerebral cortices that mark our human brains as (perhaps) uniquely able to change and adapt consciously.

Change and adaptation, in the past, have been ruled by the blind forces of supply and demand. If the grass is plentiful and the rabbits proliferate, the foxes have more food and the foxes proliferate. So the foxes eat more rabbits and the rabbit numbers fall. Back and forth, it has always gone. And this same law binds us too. If our numbers grow too large for the carrying capacity of the Earth, we shall die in droves. But these brains we have now give us, for the first time, the ability to ensure our own survival by intentionally and deliberately changing our behavior. Downshifting is a sign, therefore, of a whole new leap in the evolution of our species.

Understanding ourselves to be part of the planet and downshifting our way of living to bring ourselves into line with that understanding renders each one of us the 'fittest' for survival. Ours is the way of the future.

Chapter 7

All the nitty-gritty bits

Most books about downshifting focus on all the practical stuff. Just as most books, articles, websites and blogs that have to do with 'green' lifestyles seem to focus almost exclusively on the practicalities of a green way of being in the world.

They tell us how to go about setting up—or tapping onto—alternative energy systems such as wind and solar power.

They tell us how to use as few non-renewable resources as we can, e.g. by walking, riding a bicycle, using public transport instead of driving a car and especially by staying out of the air—which is a really important one, as air travel is one of the main ways we use up precious oil and create pollution.

They tell us all about those very important 'R' words: how to reduce, reuse, repair, recycle just about anything.

They tell us how to manage on less money. That's a big subject.[11]

It may necessitate drastic changes like moving to a smaller house. But more often, the books explain that we can save much more expense than we realize by making smaller changes than that. For instance:

By changing the way we eat
That means eating at home rather than going out and cooking tasty dishes from scratch with simple ingredients instead of buying ready meals. And it means choosing fruit and vegetables that are in season because that is when they are the cheapest.[12]

By cutting down on travel
For example by taking vacations nearer to home, cycling to work,

working from home, car-pooling.

By relearning a lot of old skills

Which means we can then do for ourselves some of the things our grandparents used to do, like growing our own food, making our own clothes and darning our socks

And it means we can make things such as gifts and cards ourselves instead of buying them so that Christmas won't make big dents in our credit cards.

The books give us lots and lots of wonderful, creative ideas for how to simplify just about everything in our lives.

The thing they do best is to tell us how to deal with 'stuff'. They do that in the following ways:

By explaining how to go about decluttering

That means getting rid of all the surplus belongings that take up space in our lives, either so that we have fewer things to clean and dust and insure and worry about or so that we can move to a smaller house.

By encouraging us to stop buying unnecessary items

That means weaning ourselves from the addiction to shopping and learning to distinguish between:

basic needs (like food and water and somewhere to live and
    enough clothing and fuel to keep us warm in winter),
lifestyle needs that will support our downshifting (such as a
    bicycle, a solar panel, a trowel, some vegetable seeds),
wants (everything else that might take our fancy).

By giving us all those super-important guidelines for how to 'buy green'

That means sourcing as much as possible of our food from our local area (growing our own in a garden, an allotment or containers on the patio, shopping at farmers' markets and farm shops, avoiding imported food items as much as we can).

It means keeping as much as possible of our money in the local economy (e.g. by buying food from local stores and co-operatives instead of supermarkets, supporting local artists, craftspeople and tradespeople, bartering, joining a LETS scheme if there is one around).

It also means thinking about social justice and avoiding any purchase that is going to harm or exploit other people anywhere in the world (e.g. by looking for the Fair Trade logo, joining boycotts of exploitative companies, refusing to buy clothing made in sweatshops).

And it means thinking about non-renewable resources such as oil and choosing purchases that have used as little of it as possible (e.g. by avoiding items that have been flown in from somewhere else, such as cut flowers or out-of-season fruit and vegetables).

By teaching us about pollution and how to protect the environment

That means we must learn about all the polluting substances that surround us and how to recognize them, avoid them and make sure we don't contribute to spreading them around. Which we can do by:

buying or using only natural products, e.g. soaps, detergents, cosmetics etc made without petrochemicals such as synthetic perfumes and preservatives,
wearing clothes made with natural fibers,
sending as little as possible to the landfill,
using only absolutely essential medication and nothing with hormones in it that will end up in the sewage system, such as birth control pills.

It means that if possible we need to grow our food organically or at least support local—preferably organic—growers.

It means using non-polluting ways of staying warm and generating energy and especially it means reducing our flying to the bare minimum, since the exhaust from airplanes is particularly damaging to the atmosphere.

It means eating a largely vegetarian diet, since the meat industry is a major contributor to the excess of carbon dioxide and methane that is causing climate change.

Whilst the books on downshifting, decluttering and simplifying are all useful in some way—some very much so—many of the green websites and blogs that I see on the Internet seem to focus almost exclusively on green *purchasing*.

Of course, if we need to buy stuff it is very helpful to know which stuff is the greenest. The alternatives need to be widely known so that everyone can choose wisely. Unfortunately, I think there is a real sense in which, by using all the power of modern advertising (and the ease of convenience of Internet retailing) many companies are tempting us merely to repaint our consumerist lifestyles in an attractive shade of green rather than replacing them with genuinely sustainable ones. Under a capitalist system, this may be inevitable. But potential downshifters do need to be vigilant.

Looking back over these last few pages, it is easy to imagine that many people who are in the early stages of thinking about downshifting might be put off by seeing a list of all the changes they might have to make to achieve that goal. Changing one's habits is often difficult. And if you glance back over the list it might look as though there is a lot of giving up involved.

Mind you, most of those who successfully manage to do it remain ever grateful that they did. For as I pointed out in earlier chapters, downshifting is not only a practical change; it is at heart a spiritual change. And when we change our outer lives, our inner lives tend to change in subtle ways as well.

So in fact there is a chicken and egg aspect to downshifting. Which comes first, the practical, green chicken or the green, spiritual egg?

From my own experience of living lightly and greenly on the Earth, researching the topic and writing books about it, I am well aware that, even for people who have had little interest in spiritual matters, living a simple, sustainable lifestyle often seems to lead to a deeper kind of spirituality. It is what inevitably happens when you slow down, spend more time outdoors, start growing things and composting and coming more into tune with the natural cycle of the seasons and Earth's own biorhythms.

At the same time, a spirituality that is based, not on dreams of some imaginal heaven above the clouds but on a reverence for—and deep connection with—our lovely planet cannot but lead a person towards living a greener, more sustainable lifestyle.

So it can happen either way and maybe it does not matter which way it happens for any given individual as long as we are all moving in the right (green) direction.

But these days, when I write about downshifting and simplicity and living green, I still choose—as I have in this book—to emphasize the emotional and spiritual aspects even more than the practical ones, simply because those are the aspects that many other writers leave out. And the spirituality I encourage is one that is either based on—or at least includes—a deep love of the Earth. We all know that the things we may find difficult or challenging to do are always much easier when we are doing them out of love for someone else. In the same way, I believe that downshifting is much easier to do when you are motivated by love of the Earth rather that by a set of 'oughts' and 'shoulds.'

The Seven Key Principles of Downshifting

There are two main ways of encouraging people to change. One is to give them a big book of rules to cover every possible situation. The other is to give them a handful of guiding principles and trust their intelligence in applying them.

I prefer the latter method, for it seems to me that once we totally understand the principle of something, then sorting out the practicalities of applying it is pretty easy.

These are the seven key principles I have presented in this book.

1. The Gaia Principle

The energies of the planet are *our* energies. We are part of Nature and fully subject to its laws. Those laws are our own laws and they rule us, no matter what elaborate religious fantasies we construct. We are a part of the Earth: cells in her living body. Whatever we do to her, we do to ourselves. When we learn to tune in to her inherent wisdom, we shall never have to ponder about right and wrong, ever again. It becomes self-evident. So when we place the wellbeing of our planet at the center of everything, we create a rule of thumb for ourselves that will work in every situation. It is like a magnet that will always point to true north. When we put Nature's needs (and remember that includes our own true needs) above our culturally-induced wants, we shall always, unerringly make the right choices in our daily lives, both individually and collectively.

2. The Autonomy Principle

This is the principle of thinking autonomously. In other words, unhooking our minds, in every possible way, from the commercially-induced 'groupthink' of the mainstream culture that powers mindless consumerism and perpetuates the 'emulative consumption' that has driven up the footprint averages.

3. The First Delphic Principle

This is the 'Know Thyself' principle of looking into ourselves, consulting our inner Parent, Adult and Child, considering our feelings and the feelings of others, getting in touch with our deepest values, beliefs, and fears and consecrating our lives to something greater and more important than our egos.

4. The Second Delphic Principle

'Nothing in Excess'. This one, also written on those ancient stone walls in Delphi, is of course the central motto of the modern downshifter. Attend to needs, not wants.

5. The Localization Principle

Always choosing local over global whenever we can, in order to strengthen our local economies, reduce mileage and maintain the integrity of our bioregions and the individuality of our cities, towns and villages.

6. The Field of Dreams Principle ('Build It and They Will Come')

Always go for the 'alternative' structures whenever possible, whether they be the physical ones like eco-houses and farmers' markets or less tangible ones like green magazines and blogs. This way, you are helping to build the strong, new, parallel system which will in time replace the broken one.

7. The 'Say Yes to Life' Principle

This one you will find in many of the world's most profound spiritual teachings. It is probably the most important principle you will ever encounter. (And for most of us, the hardest to follow!)

We green folk may still be a minority—albeit a rapidly-growing one—but when our lives are 'all of a piece' and our beliefs, our spiritual practices and our lifestyles all line up along the same, green axis, we are an unstoppable force.

So as you set out on this journey of downshifting, do as much as you can to research the subject and also devote plenty of time and energy to researching yourself and encourage anyone else who may be sharing your journey to do the same. Some people do too little research of any kind. Many do the former kind but not the latter. The best advice I can give you is to do both and then find creative ways to fit them together. And have utter faith in the process. That way lies success.

Good luck and God/Goddess/Gaia speed!

Notes

1. If you plan to do some decluttering, read Don Aslett's book *Clutter's Last Stand: It's Time To De-Junk Your Life!* 2nd edition (Marsh Creek Press, 2005). To my mind, it is the best, the funniest and the most inspiring book on decluttering ever written.
2. Maslow, A.: *Toward a Psychology of Being* 3rd edition (Wiley, 1998)
3. My book *The Lilypad List* (see note 6) has an eco-footprint calculator in the appendix. But you can also have it worked out for you online. Go to your favorite search engine and enter the terms 'ecological', 'footprint' and 'measure'.
4. 'New Internationalist' #433 (June 2010) p.17
5. Veblen, T.: *The Theory of the Leisure Class* (Oxford World's Classics) Oxford University Press, USA (January 11, 2008)
6. McCain, M.V.: *The Lilypad List: 7 steps to the simple life* (Findhorn Press, 2004)
7. First published more than forty years ago, Eric Berne's classic *Games People Play* (Ballantine, 1996) has sold over five million copies and is still widely recognized as the most original and influential popular psychology book of our times.
8. Grabill, J: *Green Kingdom Come! Jesus and a Sustainable Earth Community* (Wheatmark, 2009)
9. Andrews, C.: *The Circle of Simplicity: Return to the Good Life* (Harper Paperbacks, 1998)
10. There are many ways, nowadays, to find other 'green-minded' people, especially online. There are millions of us. The best keywords to use when you are searching, e.g. on Facebook or Yahoo Groups are 'downshifting', 'simple living', 'simplicity' and 'green living'. If you are lucky, there may be groups in your neighborhood. Check whether the 'Transition Town' movement has reached your area yet. (Do

a search on 'Transition Town' plus the name of your town or city.) You could consider starting your own downshifting support group. It is easy, and Cecile Andrews offers guidelines for doing this (see note 9). Post a notice in your local health food store and on community noticeboards, describing the sort of group you would like to start. Someone is sure to respond.

11. The classic book on the subject of managing on less money (which has never been bettered and which every downshifter probably needs to read) is *Your Money Or Your Life: 9 Steps to Transforming Your Relationship with Money and Achieving Financial Independence: Revised and Updated for the 21st Century* by Vicki Robin, Joe Dominguez and Monique Tilford (Penguin, 2008).

12. For inspiration on everything to do with food, the food industry, wholesome food, cooking from scratch and seasonality, read Michael Pollan's *The Omnivore's Dilemma* (Penguin, 2007) and Barbara Kingsolver's *Animal, Vegetable, Miracle,* written with Camille Kingsolver and Steven L. Hopp (Harper Perennial, 2008).

Other Resources

These days, the Internet is the first place to go to find out anything you want to know and to link up with like-minded individuals. But by its nature, it is—like life itself—a fluid, dynamic, ever-changing thing. So I hesitated to add URLs to this resource list. All I can say is that at the time of writing, one of the most useful websites for resources about downshifting is http://www.simpleliving.net/.

Finally, one of the best ways to learn and to be inspired in one's own endeavors is to read the personal stories of others who have done similar things. I told some of mine in *The Lilypad List* (see note 6). And another book that I really enjoyed, describes— in a highly entertaining style—the sometimes reluctant 'greening' of a UK journalist, Leo Hickman. It is entitled *A Life Stripped Bare: Tiptoeing Through the Ethical Minefield* (Transworld, 2005).

About the Author

Marian Van Eyk McCain, BSW (Melbourne), MA, East-West Psychology (C.I.I.S. San Francisco) is a retired transpersonal psychotherapist and health educator, now enjoying her incarnation as a freelance writer on a range of subjects, including wellness, simplicity, green spirituality, environmental politics, organic growing and alternative technology.

She is the author of *Transformation through Menopause* (Bergin & Garvey, 1991), the first self-help guide to the psychological, emotional and spiritual aspects of menopause, *Elderwoman: reap the wisdom, feel the power, embrace the joy* (Findhorn Press, 2002), a book for women on the 'third age' journey, and *The Lilypad List: Seven steps to the simple life* (Findhorn Press, 2004) a primer for sustainable living. She also edited the 2010 anthology *GreenSpirit: Path to a New Consciousness* (O Books, 2010) and has published several works of fiction.

Marian co-edits the 'GreenSpirit Journal', edits two newsletters and oversees several online social networks, including one for smallholders. She is also a blogger, columnist and book reviewer. A lover of all things green, she lives, very simply, in rural Devon with her soulmate and partner, Sky. She welcomes visits to her websites: www.elderwoman.org/ and www.lilypadlist.com/

Other books by Marian Van Eyk McCain

Transformation through Menopause
Elderwoman: Reap the wisdom, feel the power, embrace the joy
The Lilypad List: 7 steps to the simple life
GreenSpirit: Path to a New Consciousness (as Editor)

Fiction
Apricot Harvest
Waiting a While for Greeneyes
The Bird Menders

BOOKS

O is a symbol of the world, of oneness and unity. In different cultures it also means the "eye," symbolizing knowledge and insight. We aim to publish books that are accessible, constructive and that challenge accepted opinion, both that of academia and the "moral majority."

Our books are available in all good English language bookstores worldwide. If you don't see the book on the shelves ask the bookstore to order it for you, quoting the ISBN number and title. Alternatively you can order online (all major online retail sites carry our titles) or contact the distributor in the relevant country, listed on the copyright page.

See our website www.o-books.net for a full list of over 500 titles, growing by 100 a year.

And tune in to myspiritradio.com for our book review radio show, hosted by June-Elleni Laine, where you can listen to the authors discussing their books.

mySpiritRadio